The Wealth Effect

Unveiling the Importance of Money in Your Life.

Unlock the secrets of financial abundance and discover the profound impact money has on every aspect of your life in "The Wealth Effect: Unveiling the Importance of Money in Your Life." This compelling guide delves into the intricate relationship between money and happiness, success, relationships, health, and overall well-being. Whether you're striving for financial independence, seeking to enhance your quality of life, or aiming to redefine your relationship with money, this book provides invaluable insights and actionable strategies to empower you on your journey to prosperity.

Book Introduction:

In a world where money is both revered and reviled, its significance in our lives cannot be overstated. From the pursuit of material comforts to the fulfillment of our deepest desires, money permeates every aspect of our existence, shaping our aspirations, influencing our decisions, and defining our sense of worth. "The Wealth Effect: Unveiling the Importance of Money in Your Life" embarks on a transformative journey to illuminate the profound impact of money on our journey through life. With over 18 insightful chapters, this book offers a comprehensive exploration of the multifaceted relationship between money and human experience, guiding you toward a deeper understanding of wealth and its implications for personal fulfillment and societal well-being.

Chapter 1: Understanding the Psychology of Money

Money isn't just a medium of exchange; it's a powerful symbol that carries immense psychological weight. In this chapter, we delve into the intricate dynamics of our relationship with money, exploring the subconscious beliefs, attitudes, and behaviors that shape our financial reality. From childhood experiences to societal influences, we uncover the origins of our money mindset and its profound implications for our financial health and overall well-being. Through illuminating anecdotes and compelling research, we unravel the mysteries of human behavior and reveal the hidden drivers behind our financial decisions. Whether you're a spender, saver, or somewhere in between, this chapter offers invaluable insights to help you decode the psychology of money and unlock your path to financial abundance.

Money is a ubiquitous force in our lives, woven intricately into the fabric of society and influencing nearly every aspect of human existence. Yet, its significance extends far beyond its tangible value as a medium of exchange. Money holds immense power over our thoughts, emotions, and behaviors, shaping our perceptions, motivations, and aspirations. In this chapter, we embark on a profound exploration of the psychology of money, seeking to unravel the complex web of beliefs, attitudes, and emotions that underpin our relationship with wealth.

The Origins of Our Money Mindset

Our attitudes toward money are deeply rooted in our past experiences, beginning from the earliest stages of our development. Childhood is a crucial period during which our perceptions of money are shaped by the attitudes and behaviors of our caregivers, as well as our socioeconomic environment.

For some, money may be associated with security, abundance, and comfort, instilling a sense of confidence and empowerment. Conversely, others may grow up in environments where money is scarce, leading to feelings of anxiety, deprivation, and insecurity.

The Influence of Society and Culture

Beyond our individual experiences, societal and cultural factors play a significant role in shaping our relationship with money. From the media and advertising to societal norms and values, we are bombarded with messages that perpetuate certain beliefs about wealth and success. In many cultures, material possessions are equated with status and social worth, leading individuals to pursue wealth as a means of validation and acceptance. Moreover, societal expectations and pressure to achieve financial success can create a sense of urgency and competition, driving individuals to prioritize monetary gain above all else.

Money and Identity

Our relationship with money is deeply intertwined with our sense of self-identity and worth. For some, financial success serves as a source of pride and validation, reinforcing feelings of self-esteem and accomplishment. Conversely, others may equate their net worth with their intrinsic value as individuals, leading to feelings of inadequacy or unworthiness in the absence of wealth. Moreover, societal standards of beauty, success, and happiness often perpetuate the myth that financial wealth is synonymous with personal fulfillment, further complicating our relationship with money and identity.

The Emotional Dimensions of Wealth

Money elicits a myriad of emotions, ranging from joy and excitement to fear and anxiety. The pursuit of wealth can evoke feelings of ambition, determination, and optimism, driving individuals to strive for success and financial independence. However, the fear of loss, failure, or financial instability can also trigger feelings of stress, insecurity, and despair. Moreover, the emotional attachment to money can lead to irrational decision-making, as individuals may prioritize short-term gratification over long-term financial security.

Cognitive Biases and Financial Decision-Making

Human beings are susceptible to a variety of cognitive biases that influence our perceptions and decision-making processes. When it comes to money, these biases can have profound implications for our financial behavior and outcomes. For example, the availability heuristic may lead individuals to overestimate the likelihood of certain financial outcomes based on recent or vivid experiences, while the anchoring effect can cause individuals to rely too heavily on initial information when making financial decisions. Moreover, the endowment effect can lead individuals to place greater value on items they already possess, leading to irrational attachment and reluctance to part with them.

Breaking Free from Limiting Beliefs

To cultivate a healthy relationship with money, it is essential to challenge and reframe our limiting beliefs and attitudes surrounding wealth. By examining the underlying beliefs and emotions that drive our financial behavior, we can gain greater insight into our motivations and values. Moreover, practicing mindfulness and self-awareness can help us cultivate a more balanced perspective on money, allowing us to make more conscious and empowered financial decisions.

In conclusion, the psychology of money is a complex and multifaceted phenomenon that influences every aspect of our lives. By understanding the origins of our money mindset, the influence of societal and cultural factors, and the emotional dimensions of wealth, we can begin to unravel the intricate web of beliefs and attitudes that shape our relationship with money. Moreover, by recognizing and challenging our cognitive biases and limiting beliefs, we can cultivate a more empowered and fulfilling relationship with wealth, leading to greater financial well-being and overall satisfaction in life.

Chapter 2: The Role of Money in Achieving Dreams

Money has long been hailed as a tool for realizing our dreams and aspirations, serving as a means to an end in the pursuit of a better life. In this chapter, we delve deep into the intricate relationship between money and the fulfillment of our deepest desires, exploring the ways in which financial resources can empower us to pursue our dreams and create a life of abundance.

The Power of Financial Freedom

Financial freedom lies at the heart of our ability to pursue our dreams with confidence and conviction. When we are no longer shackled by the constraints of financial insecurity or debt, we are free to explore our passions, pursue our interests, and invest in our personal growth and development. Moreover, financial freedom provides us with the flexibility and autonomy to make choices that align with our values and priorities, allowing us to live life on our own terms.

Investing in Yourself

One of the most powerful ways in which money can help us achieve our dreams is by investing in ourselves. Whether through education, skill development, or personal enrichment activities, investing in ourselves lays the foundation for personal and professional growth. By acquiring new knowledge, honing our talents, and expanding our horizons, we can unlock new opportunities and realize our full potential. Moreover, investing in ourselves not only enhances our skills and abilities but also boosts our confidence and self-esteem, empowering us to pursue our dreams with determination and resilience.

Pursuing Passion Projects

For many of us, our dreams are intrinsically tied to our passions and interests. Whether it's starting a business, writing a book, or traveling the world, pursuing our passion projects often requires financial resources to get off the ground. Money can provide the necessary capital to fund our endeavors, whether through startup funding, equipment and materials, or marketing and promotion. Moreover, having financial resources at our disposal can alleviate the stress and uncertainty associated with pursuing our dreams, allowing us to focus on what truly matters: bringing our vision to life.

Creating Opportunities for Others

Beyond fulfilling our own dreams, money also has the power to create opportunities for others. Whether through philanthropy, mentorship, or investing in community initiatives, we can use our financial resources to uplift and empower those around us. By giving back to our communities and supporting causes that are meaningful to us, we can make a positive impact on the lives of others and contribute to the greater good. Moreover, by fostering a culture of generosity and compassion, we inspire others to pay it forward, creating a ripple effect of positive change that extends far beyond our own sphere of influence.

Overcoming Financial Barriers

Despite the inherent power of money to facilitate the pursuit of our dreams, financial barriers can often stand in our way. From limited access to capital to systemic barriers that perpetuate inequality, many individuals face significant obstacles on their journey to realizing their dreams. However, by leveraging creativity, resourcefulness, and resilience, we can overcome these barriers and find alternative pathways to success. Whether through crowdfunding, collaboration, or seeking out unconventional funding sources, there are myriad ways to navigate financial challenges and pursue our dreams against all odds.

Cultivating a Wealth Mindset

At its core, achieving our dreams is not just about accumulating wealth; it's about cultivating a mindset of abundance and possibility. By adopting a wealth mindset, we shift our focus from scarcity to abundance, recognizing the limitless potential that exists within us and in the world around us. Moreover, by embracing gratitude, optimism, and a belief in our own worthiness, we open ourselves up to a wealth of opportunities and experiences that can enrich our lives in ways we never thought possible.

In conclusion, the role of money in achieving our dreams is multifaceted and profound. From providing the resources necessary to pursue our passions to creating opportunities for others and overcoming financial barriers, money serves as a powerful catalyst for realizing our deepest desires. By leveraging our financial resources wisely, investing in ourselves and others, and cultivating a mindset of abundance, we can unlock our full potential and create a life of purpose, fulfillment, and abundance.

Chapter 3: Money and Mental Health: Breaking the Stigma

Money and mental health are two interconnected aspects of human well-being that often intersect in profound and complex ways. In this chapter, we explore the intricate relationship between finances and mental health, shedding light on the impact of financial stressors on mental well-being, the stigma surrounding mental health issues, and strategies for promoting financial and psychological resilience.

Understanding the Link Between Money and Mental Health

Financial well-being and mental health are closely intertwined, with each exerting a significant influence on the other. Financial stressors, such as debt, unemployment, or financial instability, can take a toll on one's mental health, leading to feelings of anxiety, depression, and hopelessness. Conversely, individuals struggling with mental health issues may find it challenging to manage their finances effectively, leading to further financial strain and exacerbating existing mental health symptoms. Moreover, the stigma surrounding mental health can create barriers to seeking help and support, perpetuating a cycle of financial and psychological distress.

The Impact of Financial Stress on Mental Health

Financial stress is a pervasive and often overlooked source of mental health problems, affecting individuals across all socioeconomic backgrounds. Whether it's struggling to make ends meet, facing mounting debt, or experiencing job loss or financial insecurity, the burden of financial stress can be overwhelming and debilitating. Studies have shown that individuals experiencing financial difficulties are at a higher risk of developing mental health disorders, such as anxiety and depression, and are more likely to engage in unhealthy coping mechanisms, such as substance abuse or avoidance behaviors. Moreover, the chronic stress associated with financial problems can take a toll on physical health, leading to increased risk of chronic diseases and other adverse health outcomes.

Challenging the Stigma Surrounding Mental Health

Despite growing awareness and advocacy efforts, mental health stigma remains a pervasive barrier to seeking help and support. The fear of judgment, discrimination, or social exclusion often prevents individuals from disclosing their mental health struggles or seeking treatment, leading to feelings of shame, isolation, and self-stigma. Moreover, cultural and societal attitudes toward mental illness can perpetuate misconceptions and stereotypes, further marginalizing individuals with mental health disorders and impeding their access to care. Breaking the stigma surrounding mental health requires collective action and cultural change, including destigmatizing conversations around mental illness, promoting empathy and understanding, and advocating for accessible and inclusive mental health services.

Strategies for Promoting Financial and Psychological Resilience

Building resilience in the face of financial and mental health challenges requires a multifaceted approach that addresses both individual and systemic factors. From a financial perspective, cultivating financial literacy and management skills can empower individuals to make informed decisions and navigate financial challenges more effectively. This may include budgeting, saving, and investing strategies, as well as seeking professional financial advice and support when needed. Additionally, fostering a supportive and inclusive workplace culture that prioritizes employee well-being and offers resources and support for mental health can help reduce stigma and create a more psychologically healthy work environment.

Seeking Help and Support

Above all, it's essential for individuals experiencing financial or mental health difficulties to know that help and support are available. Whether through therapy, counseling, financial coaching, or peer support groups, there are numerous resources and services available to help individuals navigate financial and mental health challenges and build resilience. It's okay to reach out for help, and seeking support is a sign of strength, not weakness. By breaking the silence and stigma surrounding money and mental health, we can create a more compassionate and supportive society where everyone has the opportunity to thrive.

In conclusion, the relationship between money and mental health is complex and multifaceted, with each exerting a significant influence on the other. Financial stressors can exacerbate mental health problems, while mental health issues can impact one's ability to manage finances effectively. By challenging the stigma surrounding mental health, promoting financial literacy and resilience, and fostering a culture of support and understanding, we can break down barriers to seeking help and create a more inclusive and compassionate society where everyone has the opportunity to live a healthy and fulfilling life.

Chapter 4: Financial Literacy: The Key to Economic Empowerment

Financial literacy is widely recognized as a fundamental skill for navigating the complexities of modern life and achieving economic empowerment. In this chapter, we delve into the importance of financial literacy, exploring its impact on individual and societal well-being, the challenges to promoting financial education, and strategies for improving financial literacy across diverse populations.

Understanding Financial Literacy

Financial literacy refers to the knowledge, skills, and competencies necessary to make informed financial decisions and effectively manage one's finances. It encompasses a wide range of topics, including budgeting, saving, investing, debt management, and understanding financial products and services. Financially literate individuals are equipped with the tools and resources needed to navigate complex financial systems, plan for the future, and achieve their financial goals.

The Importance of Financial Literacy

Financial literacy is a critical component of economic empowerment, enabling individuals to take control of their financial futures and build a solid foundation for long-term financial well-being. By understanding basic financial concepts and principles, individuals can make informed decisions about spending, saving, and investing, thereby reducing the risk of financial insecurity and improving their overall financial health. Moreover, financial literacy empowers individuals to advocate for their own interests, negotiate financial transactions, and access essential financial services, such as banking, credit, and insurance.

The Impact of Financial Illiteracy

Conversely, a lack of financial literacy can have serious consequences for individuals and society as a whole. Without the necessary knowledge and skills to manage their finances effectively, individuals may fall prey to predatory lending practices, accumulate high levels of debt, or make uninformed investment decisions, leading to financial hardship and instability. Moreover, financial illiteracy perpetuates cycles of poverty and inequality, as individuals from disadvantaged backgrounds may lack access to quality financial education and resources, further exacerbating socioeconomic disparities.

Challenges to Promoting Financial Education

Despite the importance of financial literacy, there are numerous challenges to promoting financial education and empowerment. Limited access to quality financial education programs, inadequate resources and support for educators, and competing demands on individuals' time and attention are just a few of the barriers that hinder efforts to improve financial literacy. Moreover, cultural and societal factors, such as stigma surrounding financial issues or cultural taboos around discussing money, can further complicate efforts to promote financial education and awareness.

Strategies for Improving Financial Literacy

Addressing the challenges of financial literacy requires a multifaceted approach that involves collaboration between governments, educational institutions, employers, and community organizations. Investing in financial education programs and resources, integrating financial literacy into school curricula, and providing targeted support and resources for vulnerable populations are essential steps toward improving financial literacy and empowering individuals to make informed financial decisions. Moreover, leveraging technology and digital platforms can expand access to financial education and services, reaching individuals who may be underserved or marginalized by traditional financial institutions.

Empowering Individuals Through Financial Education

Ultimately, financial literacy is about more than just managing money; it's about empowering individuals to take control of their financial futures and achieve their dreams. By equipping individuals with the knowledge, skills, and resources needed to make informed financial decisions, we can create a more financially secure and prosperous society for all. Through education, advocacy, and collaboration, we can break down barriers to financial literacy and empower individuals to build brighter futures for themselves and their communities.

In conclusion, financial literacy is a powerful tool for promoting economic empowerment and improving individual and societal well-being. By understanding the importance of financial literacy, addressing the challenges to promoting financial education, and implementing strategies for improving financial literacy, we can empower individuals to take control of their financial futures and achieve their goals. Together, we can build a more inclusive and prosperous society where everyone has the opportunity to thrive.

Chapter 5: Navigating Relationships in the Realm of Wealth

Navigating relationships in the realm of wealth is a multifaceted endeavor that requires sensitivity, communication, and mutual understanding. In this chapter, we delve into the complexities of how money influences relationships, from romantic partnerships and family dynamics to friendships and professional networks. We explore the challenges and opportunities that arise when wealth enters the equation, as well as strategies for fostering healthy, fulfilling relationships in the context of financial abundance.

The Impact of Wealth on Relationships

Wealth can profoundly impact relationships, shaping dynamics, power structures, and communication patterns. In romantic partnerships, financial disparities can lead to tension, resentment, and conflicts over money management and spending habits. Similarly, within families, issues related to inheritance, wealth distribution, and financial expectations can strain relationships and lead to feelings of entitlement or jealousy among siblings and extended family members. Moreover, friendships and professional networks may be influenced by wealth disparities, with individuals gravitating toward others of similar financial means or feeling uncomfortable discussing money-related topics.

Communicating Effectively About Money

Open, honest communication is essential for navigating relationships in the realm of wealth. Couples and families should establish clear channels of communication around financial matters, including budgeting, saving, investing, and long-term financial goals. This may involve setting regular check-ins to discuss finances, establishing shared financial goals, and creating a sense of transparency and accountability around money management. Moreover, individuals should feel empowered to communicate their needs, boundaries, and concerns related to money, fostering mutual understanding and respect within relationships.

Managing Conflicts and Resentment

Conflicts and resentments can arise when wealth disparities are not addressed or when individuals feel misunderstood or undervalued in their relationships. It's essential to approach conflicts with empathy, compassion, and a willingness to listen and understand each other's perspectives. Couples and families may benefit from seeking professional guidance from financial advisors, therapists, or mediators to navigate complex financial issues and resolve conflicts in a constructive manner. Moreover, practicing gratitude, appreciation, and generosity can help mitigate feelings of resentment and foster a sense of connection and solidarity within relationships.

Setting Boundaries and Expectations

Setting clear boundaries and expectations around money is crucial for maintaining healthy, balanced relationships. Couples and families should discuss and establish shared values and priorities related to money, such as saving for retirement, investing in education, or supporting charitable causes. Additionally, individuals should feel empowered to set personal boundaries around financial matters, such as loaning money to friends or family members, managing financial obligations, and protecting their own financial security. Establishing boundaries helps prevent misunderstandings and conflicts and fosters trust and respect within relationships.

Cultivating Financial Intimacy

Financial intimacy involves sharing openly and vulnerably about money within relationships, fostering a sense of trust, connection, and partnership. Couples and families can cultivate financial intimacy by discussing their financial histories, goals, fears, and dreams, as well as sharing responsibility for financial decision-making and planning. This may involve joint budgeting, saving, and investing, as well as setting shared financial goals and milestones. Cultivating financial intimacy creates a sense of shared purpose and collaboration within relationships, strengthening bonds and deepening emotional connection.

Fostering Empathy and Understanding

Empathy and understanding are essential for navigating relationships in the realm of wealth. Individuals should strive to understand each other's perspectives, experiences, and emotions related to money, recognizing that financial decisions are often influenced by personal values, beliefs, and past experiences. Practicing empathy involves active listening, validation, and validation, as well as offering support and encouragement to each other in times of financial challenge or uncertainty. By fostering empathy and understanding within relationships, individuals can build stronger, more resilient bonds that withstand the tests of time and financial adversity.

In conclusion, navigating relationships in the realm of wealth requires compassion, communication, and collaboration. By fostering open, honest communication, managing conflicts and resentments, setting boundaries and expectations, cultivating financial intimacy, and fostering empathy and understanding, individuals can build healthy, fulfilling relationships that thrive in the context of financial abundance. Through mutual respect, trust, and support, individuals can navigate the complexities of wealth and relationships with grace and resilience, fostering deeper connections and greater happiness and satisfaction in life.

Chapter 6: The Impact of Money on Physical Health

Money has a profound influence on many aspects of our lives, including our physical health. In this chapter, we delve into the complex relationship between money and physical well-being, exploring how socioeconomic factors, access to healthcare, lifestyle choices, and stress levels all intersect to shape our health outcomes. From disparities in healthcare access to the physiological effects of financial stress, we examine the various ways in which money impacts our bodies and overall physical health.

Socioeconomic Disparities in Health Outcomes

Socioeconomic status is a significant determinant of health outcomes, with individuals from lower socioeconomic backgrounds experiencing higher rates of chronic diseases, disabilities, and premature mortality. Economic inequalities, including disparities in income, education, employment, and access to resources, contribute to differences in health outcomes among different socioeconomic groups. For example, individuals living in poverty are more likely to face barriers to accessing quality healthcare, nutritious food, safe housing, and other essential resources that are critical for maintaining good health.

Access to Healthcare and Medical Services

Access to healthcare is a crucial factor in determining health outcomes, and financial barriers can prevent individuals from receiving timely and appropriate medical care. Without adequate health insurance coverage or financial resources to pay for medical expenses, individuals may delay seeking necessary healthcare services, forego preventive care, or ration medications, leading to untreated medical conditions and poorer health outcomes. Moreover, disparities in healthcare access and quality contribute to health inequities, with marginalized communities facing greater challenges in accessing timely and high-quality healthcare services.

Lifestyle Choices and Health Behaviors

Financial resources play a significant role in shaping lifestyle choices and health behaviors, as individuals with higher incomes may have greater access to resources that promote health and well-being. For example, individuals with higher incomes may be able to afford gym memberships, healthy food options, recreational activities, and other wellness resources that support physical health. Conversely, individuals with limited financial resources may face barriers to adopting healthy behaviors due to cost constraints, such as the high cost of nutritious foods, exercise equipment, or transportation to recreational facilities.

The Physiological Effects of Financial Stress

Financial stress is a common experience for many individuals and can have profound effects on physical health. Chronic financial stress activates the body's stress response system, triggering the release of stress hormones like cortisol and adrenaline, which can have detrimental effects on the cardiovascular, immune, and metabolic systems. Prolonged exposure to financial stress is associated with an increased risk of hypertension, heart disease, obesity, diabetes, and other chronic health conditions. Moreover, financial stress can exacerbate mental health problems like anxiety and depression, further impacting physical well-being.

Coping Mechanisms and Health Outcomes

Individuals facing financial challenges may adopt coping mechanisms that have both positive and negative effects on their physical health. For example, some individuals may turn to unhealthy coping strategies like smoking, excessive alcohol consumption, or overeating as a way to cope with stress or alleviate negative emotions. These behaviors can increase the risk of developing chronic diseases and worsen existing health conditions. Conversely, individuals who engage in positive coping mechanisms like seeking social support, practicing stress-reduction techniques, or engaging in physical activity may experience better health outcomes despite financial challenges.

Addressing Health Inequities and Promoting Health Equity

Addressing health inequities requires a comprehensive approach that addresses the social, economic, and environmental determinants of health. This includes efforts to reduce income inequality, improve access to affordable healthcare and essential resources, and address social and environmental factors that contribute to health disparities. Moreover, promoting health equity requires recognizing and addressing systemic barriers and injustices that perpetuate health inequities, including racism, discrimination, and socioeconomic inequalities. By working collaboratively to address these factors, we can create a more equitable and just healthcare system that promotes the health and well-being of all individuals, regardless of their financial status.

In conclusion, the impact of money on physical health is multifaceted and complex, with socioeconomic factors, access to healthcare, lifestyle choices, and stress levels all playing significant roles in shaping health outcomes. By addressing health inequities, promoting access to affordable healthcare and essential resources, and addressing the root causes of financial stress, we can create a more equitable and inclusive society where everyone has the opportunity to live a healthy and fulfilling life. Through collective action and collaboration, we can work towards a future where financial security and good health are accessible to all individuals, regardless of their socioeconomic status.

Chapter 7: Money Mindset: Shifting from Scarcity to Abundance

Our mindset shapes our relationship with money in profound ways, influencing our beliefs, attitudes, and behaviors surrounding wealth and abundance. In this chapter, we explore the concept of money mindset and the transformative power of shifting from a mindset of scarcity to one of abundance. We delve into the psychological and emotional factors that contribute to scarcity mentality, examine the limitations it imposes on our lives, and offer strategies for cultivating an abundance mindset that empowers us to attract wealth and abundance into our lives.

Understanding Scarcity Mindset

Scarcity mindset is a psychological phenomenon characterized by a pervasive sense of lack, fear, and inadequacy. Individuals with a scarcity mindset view resources, including money, as finite and limited, leading to feelings of anxiety, fear, and competition. This mindset is rooted in a belief that there is not enough to go around, leading individuals to hoard resources, resist change, and engage in behaviors driven by fear and insecurity. Scarcity mindset often manifests as a fear of failure, a fear of not having enough, and a fear of missing out on opportunities.

The Limitations of Scarcity Mindset

Scarcity mindset imposes significant limitations on our ability to achieve our goals and live fulfilling lives. When we operate from a mindset of scarcity, we are constantly focused on what we lack rather than what we have, leading to feelings of frustration, discontent, and powerlessness. This narrow focus on scarcity blinds us to opportunities for growth and abundance, leading us to overlook potential solutions and resources that could help us achieve our goals. Moreover, scarcity mindset can negatively impact our relationships, leading to conflicts over money, feelings of envy or resentment, and an inability to trust or collaborate with others.

Cultivating an Abundance Mindset

Shifting from scarcity to abundance mindset involves reframing our beliefs, attitudes, and perceptions surrounding money and wealth. At its core, abundance mindset is rooted in the belief that there is more than enough to go around and that we have the power to create and attract abundance into our lives. Cultivating an abundance mindset involves adopting a mindset of gratitude, abundance, and possibility, focusing on what we have rather than what we lack, and embracing opportunities for growth and expansion. It also involves releasing limiting beliefs and fears surrounding money and wealth, such as beliefs about unworthiness, scarcity, or the need to compete for resources.

Practicing Gratitude and Appreciation

Gratitude is a powerful tool for shifting from scarcity to abundance mindset. By cultivating a practice of gratitude and appreciation, we train our minds to focus on the abundance that already exists in our lives, rather than fixating on what we lack. This practice involves acknowledging and expressing gratitude for the blessings, opportunities, and resources that we have, whether big or small. By shifting our focus from scarcity to abundance, we open ourselves up to a wealth of possibilities and opportunities for growth and expansion.

Embracing a Growth Mindset

Embracing a growth mindset is another key component of cultivating abundance mindset. A growth mindset is characterized by a belief in our ability to learn, grow, and adapt in the face of challenges and setbacks. By adopting a growth mindset, we view challenges as opportunities for growth and learning, rather than insurmountable obstacles. This mindset empowers us to take risks, embrace change, and pursue our goals with confidence and resilience. Moreover, by recognizing our own potential for growth and success, we attract opportunities for abundance into our lives and create a positive feedback loop of growth and expansion.

Affirmations and Visualization

Affirmations and visualization are powerful tools for reprogramming our subconscious minds and aligning our thoughts and beliefs with our desires. Affirmations are positive statements or declarations that affirm our desired outcomes or beliefs, such as "I am worthy of abundance" or "I attract wealth and prosperity into my life." By repeating these affirmations regularly, we reinforce positive beliefs and attitudes surrounding money and abundance, thereby shifting our mindset from scarcity to abundance. Visualization involves mentally picturing our desired outcomes or experiences, allowing us to create a vivid mental image of the abundant future we wish to create. By visualizing our goals and desires with clarity and intention, we activate the law of attraction and attract the resources and opportunities needed to manifest our dreams into reality.

Taking Inspired Action

Finally, shifting from scarcity to abundance mindset involves taking inspired action towards our goals and desires. This involves stepping out of our comfort zones, taking calculated risks, and pursuing our goals with intention and determination. By aligning our thoughts, beliefs, and actions with our desires, we signal to the universe our readiness to receive abundance and create the life of our dreams. Taking inspired action involves trusting our intuition, following our passions, and remaining open to the opportunities and synchronicities that arise along the way.

Conclusion

In conclusion, shifting from scarcity to abundance mindset is a transformative journey that empowers us to attract wealth and abundance into our lives. By releasing limiting beliefs and fears surrounding money, practicing gratitude and appreciation, embracing a growth mindset, and taking inspired action towards our goals, we create a positive energetic vibration that attracts abundance and prosperity into our lives. Through the power of mindset, we can unlock our true potential, manifest our deepest desires, and create a life of abundance, joy, and fulfillment.

Chapter 8: Investing in Yourself: Personal Development and Wealth

Investing in yourself is one of the most valuable investments you can make. In this chapter, we explore the concept of personal development as a pathway to wealth and fulfillment. We delve into the various ways in which investing in yourself can lead to personal and financial growth, including developing new skills, nurturing your talents, expanding your knowledge, and prioritizing self-care. By committing to your personal growth and development, you not only enhance your earning potential but also enrich your life in profound ways.

Recognizing the Value of Self-Investment

Investing in yourself is an investment in your future and your overall well-being. By allocating time, resources, and energy towards your personal growth and development, you lay the foundation for long-term success and fulfillment. Whether it's pursuing higher education, acquiring new skills, or investing in experiences that nourish your mind, body, and soul, self-investment enables you to unlock your full potential and create a life that aligns with your values, passions, and aspirations.

Developing New Skills and Expertise

One of the most effective ways to invest in yourself is by continuously developing new skills and expertise. In today's rapidly evolving world, staying relevant and adaptable is essential for success in any field. By investing in lifelong learning and skill development, you enhance your marketability, increase your earning potential, and open up new opportunities for career advancement and growth. Whether it's taking courses, attending workshops, or pursuing certifications, committing to ongoing skill development enables you to stay ahead of the curve and thrive in a competitive marketplace.

Nurturing Your Talents and Passions

Investing in yourself also involves nurturing your talents and passions, those innate gifts and interests that bring you joy and fulfillment. Whether it's pursuing a creative hobby, starting a side hustle, or launching a passion project, investing time and energy into activities that ignite your passion enables you to cultivate your unique talents and express your authentic self. Moreover, by aligning your passions with your professional pursuits, you can create a career that feels meaningful, purposeful, and deeply fulfilling.

Expanding Your Knowledge and Perspective

Expanding your knowledge and perspective is another valuable form of self-investment. By exposing yourself to new ideas, perspectives, and experiences, you broaden your horizons, deepen your understanding of the world, and cultivate empathy and compassion for others. Whether it's reading books, listening to podcasts, or traveling to new places, investing in experiences that challenge and expand your worldview enables you to become a more well-rounded, informed, and culturally competent individual.

Prioritizing Self-Care and Well-Being

Self-care is an essential aspect of self-investment, as it enables you to prioritize your physical, emotional, and mental well-being. Investing in self-care practices such as exercise, meditation, mindfulness, and healthy eating nourishes your mind, body, and spirit, enabling you to show up as your best self in all areas of your life. By prioritizing self-care, you enhance your resilience, reduce stress and burnout, and cultivate a greater sense of balance, fulfillment, and joy.

Building Resilience and Adaptability

Investing in yourself also involves building resilience and adaptability, the ability to bounce back from setbacks and navigate change with grace and resilience. By embracing challenges as opportunities for growth and learning, you develop the resilience to overcome obstacles and setbacks on your path to success. Moreover, by cultivating a growth mindset and embracing change as a natural part of life, you become more adaptable and resourceful in the face of uncertainty and adversity.

Conclusion

In conclusion, investing in yourself is one of the most powerful investments you can make. By committing to your personal growth and development, you unlock your full potential, enhance your earning potential, and create a life of abundance and fulfillment. Whether it's developing new skills, nurturing your talents, expanding your knowledge, or prioritizing self-care, investing in yourself enables you to become the best version of yourself and create a life that reflects your values, passions, and aspirations. Through self-investment, you empower yourself to achieve your goals, overcome obstacles, and live a life of purpose, meaning, and joy.

Chapter 9: Building Generational Wealth: Securing Your Legacy

Building generational wealth is about more than just accumulating money; it's about creating a lasting legacy that provides financial security and opportunities for future generations. In this chapter, we explore the principles and strategies for building generational wealth, including investment strategies, estate planning, financial education, and fostering a mindset of abundance and stewardship. By taking intentional action to build and preserve wealth, you can leave a lasting impact on your family and future generations for years to come.

Understanding Generational Wealth

Generational wealth refers to assets and resources that are passed down from one generation to the next, providing financial security and opportunities for future descendants. Unlike temporary wealth, which may be spent or depleted within a single generation, generational wealth is intended to be preserved and grown over time, ensuring a lasting legacy for future generations. This wealth can take many forms, including financial assets, real estate, businesses, and intellectual property, and is often accompanied by a set of values, principles, and traditions that guide its management and distribution.

Investment Strategies for Long-Term Growth

Investment strategies play a crucial role in building generational wealth, as they enable you to grow and preserve your assets over time. Long-term investment vehicles such as stocks, bonds, mutual funds, and real estate can provide steady returns and inflation protection, helping your wealth grow exponentially over time. Additionally, diversification across asset classes and geographic regions can help mitigate risk and enhance long-term returns. By adopting a disciplined investment approach and focusing on long-term growth rather than short-term gains, you can create a solid foundation for building generational wealth.

Estate Planning and Wealth Transfer

Estate planning is a critical component of building generational wealth, as it ensures that your assets are distributed according to your wishes and that your family is financially protected in the event of your passing. Key estate planning tools include wills, trusts, and powers of attorney, which enable you to designate beneficiaries, specify asset distribution, and minimize estate taxes and probate costs. By creating a comprehensive estate plan that addresses your financial goals, values, and concerns, you can secure your legacy and provide for your loved ones for generations to come.

Financial Education and Empowerment

Financial education is essential for building generational wealth, as it equips family members with the knowledge and skills they need to manage money wisely and make informed financial decisions. Teaching children about budgeting, saving, investing, and debt management from a young age instills a sense of financial responsibility and empowers them to build wealth and achieve their goals. Moreover, ongoing financial education for adults can help family members navigate complex financial decisions, such as purchasing a home, starting a business, or planning for retirement, with confidence and competence.

Fostering a Mindset of Abundance and Stewardship

Fostering a mindset of abundance and stewardship is key to building generational wealth, as it encourages family members to view wealth as a tool for creating positive change and leaving a lasting legacy. By instilling values such as gratitude, generosity, and responsibility, you can cultivate a culture of stewardship within your family that promotes wise financial decision-making and charitable giving. Additionally, promoting open communication and collaboration among family members fosters a sense of unity and shared purpose, enabling you to work together towards common financial goals and aspirations.

Conclusion

In conclusion, building generational wealth is a multifaceted endeavor that requires careful planning, disciplined investing, and a commitment to financial education and empowerment. By adopting investment strategies for long-term growth, implementing comprehensive estate planning, prioritizing financial education and empowerment, and fostering a mindset of abundance and stewardship, you can create a lasting legacy that provides financial security and opportunities for future generations. Through intentional action and shared values, you can build generational wealth that transcends financial assets and leaves a lasting impact on your family and community for generations to come.

Chapter 10: Overcoming Financial Obstacles and Adversity

Financial obstacles and adversity are inevitable challenges that many individuals face on their journey to financial success. In this chapter, we explore the common financial obstacles that people encounter, such as debt, unemployment, unexpected expenses, and economic downturns. We delve into strategies for overcoming these obstacles and navigating financial adversity with resilience, resourcefulness, and determination. By empowering yourself with knowledge, skills, and strategies, you can overcome financial obstacles and emerge stronger and more resilient than ever before.

Understanding Financial Obstacles

Financial obstacles can take many forms, from personal challenges such as debt and low income to external factors such as economic downturns and market volatility. These obstacles can hinder your ability to achieve your financial goals and create stress, anxiety, and uncertainty. Common financial obstacles include:

- Debt: High levels of debt can be a significant obstacle to financial success, making it challenging to save, invest, or achieve other financial goals.
- Unemployment: Job loss or underemployment can disrupt your income stream and jeopardize your financial stability.
- Unexpected Expenses: Emergencies such as medical bills, car repairs, or home repairs can strain your finances and derail your financial plans.
- Economic Downturns: Economic downturns such as recessions or market crashes can impact your investments, job security, and overall financial well-being.

Strategies for Overcoming Financial Obstacles

Create a Budget: Creating a budget helps you track your income and expenses, identify areas where you can cut back, and prioritize your spending to align with your financial goals.

Reduce Debt: Develop a debt repayment plan to pay off high-interest debt systematically, such as the snowball or avalanche method. Consider consolidating debt or negotiating with creditors to lower interest rates.

Build Emergency Savings: Start building an emergency fund to cover unexpected expenses and financial emergencies. Aim to save three to six months' worth of living expenses in a separate savings account.

Diversify Income Streams: Explore opportunities to diversify your income streams, such as freelancing, consulting, or starting a side business. Having multiple sources of income can provide stability and resilience in uncertain times.

Invest Wisely: Develop a diversified investment portfolio tailored to your risk tolerance, time horizon, and financial goals. Consider working with a financial advisor to create a personalized investment strategy.

Seek Financial Education: Educate yourself about personal finance topics such as budgeting, investing, and debt management. Take advantage of free resources such as books, podcasts, and online courses to improve your financial literacy.

Practice Frugality: Adopt frugal habits such as living below your means, avoiding unnecessary expenses, and prioritizing value over luxury. Look for ways to save money on everyday expenses without sacrificing quality of life.

Stay Resilient: Cultivate a mindset of resilience and perseverance in the face of financial challenges. Focus on what you can control, adapt to changes, and seek support from friends, family, or financial professionals when needed.

Navigating Financial Adversity

Stay Calm: In times of financial adversity, it's essential to remain calm and avoid making impulsive decisions. Take a step back, assess your situation objectively, and develop a plan of action.

Assess Your Options: Evaluate your financial situation and explore potential solutions to address your challenges. Consider seeking advice from financial professionals, such as financial advisors or credit counselors, to explore all available options.

Prioritize Essential Expenses: Prioritize essential expenses such as housing, food, and utilities to ensure your basic needs are met. Cut back on non-essential expenses temporarily until you regain financial stability.

Communicate with Creditors: If you're struggling to meet your financial obligations, communicate with your creditors proactively. They may be willing to offer temporary payment arrangements or hardship assistance to help you through difficult times.

Seek Support: Don't hesitate to seek support from friends, family, or community resources if you're facing financial adversity. You're not alone, and there are resources available to help you navigate challenging times.

Focus on Long-Term Goals: Keep your long-term financial goals in mind and stay focused on taking steps to achieve them, even during periods of adversity. Maintaining a positive outlook and staying committed to your goals can help you overcome temporary setbacks and emerge stronger in the long run.

Conclusion

Overcoming financial obstacles and adversity requires resilience, resourcefulness, and determination. By adopting proactive strategies such as budgeting, debt reduction, emergency savings, and diversifying income streams, you can build financial resilience and navigate challenges with confidence. Remember that financial setbacks are temporary, and with perseverance and a positive mindset, you can overcome obstacles and achieve your financial goals. Through education, planning, and perseverance, you can emerge from financial adversity stronger and more resilient than ever before.

Chapter 11: Money and Happiness: Debunking Myths

Money and happiness are often thought to be closely linked, with many people believing that greater wealth leads to greater happiness. However, this relationship is far more complex than it may seem. In this chapter, we delve into the myths surrounding money and happiness, exploring the nuances of their relationship and uncovering the factors that truly contribute to overall well-being and life satisfaction. By debunking common myths and misconceptions, we can gain a deeper understanding of how money influences happiness and how to cultivate a more fulfilling and meaningful life.

Myth 1: More Money Equals More Happiness

One of the most pervasive myths about money and happiness is the belief that more money equals more happiness. While it's true that financial security and stability can contribute to overall well-being, research suggests that the relationship between income and happiness is more nuanced than many people assume. Studies have found that once basic needs are met, increases in income have diminishing returns on happiness, with higher levels of wealth correlating only modestly with greater life satisfaction. Additionally, the pursuit of wealth and material possessions can sometimes detract from other sources of happiness, such as meaningful relationships, personal growth, and experiences.

Myth 2: Material Possessions Bring Lasting Happiness

Another common myth is the belief that material possessions bring lasting happiness. While acquiring new possessions may provide a temporary boost in happiness, this effect tends to be short-lived. Research has shown that people adapt quickly to new possessions, and the initial excitement and satisfaction they bring often fade over time. Moreover, the pursuit of material wealth can lead to a cycle of consumerism and hedonic adaptation, where individuals continually seek out new possessions in a futile quest for lasting happiness. In contrast, experiences, relationships, and personal growth tend to have a more enduring impact on happiness and life satisfaction.

Myth 3: Wealthy People Are Happier

There is a widespread belief that wealthy people are happier than those with lower incomes. However, research has found that while wealthier individuals may report higher levels of life satisfaction than those living in poverty, the difference in happiness between middle-income and high-income individuals is relatively small. Moreover, factors such as social connections, sense of purpose, and overall well-being have a more significant impact on happiness than income alone. Wealthy individuals may face unique challenges and stressors related to their financial status, such as concerns about maintaining their wealth, managing high expectations, and navigating social pressures.

Myth 4: Financial Success Guarantees Happiness

Many people equate financial success with happiness, believing that achieving financial goals such as buying a home, earning a high salary, or attaining a certain level of wealth will lead to lasting fulfillment. However, research suggests that financial success alone does not guarantee happiness. While achieving financial goals may provide a sense of accomplishment and security, true happiness often stems from other sources, such as meaningful relationships, personal growth, and a sense of purpose. Moreover, the pursuit of financial success can sometimes come at the expense of other aspects of life, such as health, well-being, and work-life balance.

Myth 5: Happiness Is Unattainable Without Wealth

Contrary to popular belief, happiness is not contingent upon wealth or material possessions. While financial security and stability can contribute to overall well-being, happiness is ultimately a subjective experience that arises from within. Research has shown that factors such as gratitude, kindness, resilience, and social connections have a more significant impact on happiness than material wealth alone. Moreover, individuals from all walks of life, regardless of their income or socioeconomic status, have the capacity to experience happiness and fulfillment through meaningful experiences, meaningful relationships, and a sense of purpose.

Debunking the Myths: Cultivating True Happiness

Cultivating true happiness involves debunking the myths surrounding money and happiness and focusing on the factors that truly contribute to well-being and life satisfaction. Rather than chasing after material wealth or external validation, focus on cultivating inner qualities such as gratitude, compassion, resilience, and authenticity. Prioritize experiences over possessions, invest in meaningful relationships, and pursue activities that bring you joy and fulfillment. By aligning your life with your values and priorities, you can create a more fulfilling and meaningful life, regardless of your financial circumstances.

Conclusion

In conclusion, the relationship between money and happiness is far more complex than many people assume. While financial security and stability are important for overall well-being, they are not the sole determinants of happiness. By debunking the myths surrounding money and happiness and focusing on factors such as meaningful relationships, personal growth, and a sense of purpose, you can cultivate true happiness and fulfillment in your life. Remember that happiness is a journey, not a destination, and that true happiness comes from within. By prioritizing what truly matters and living in alignment with your values, you can create a life that is rich in meaning, purpose, and joy.

Chapter 12: Creating Financial Freedom Through Passive Income

Financial freedom is a goal that many aspire to achieve, allowing individuals to live life on their own terms without being constrained by financial obligations. In this chapter, we explore the concept of passive income as a pathway to financial freedom. We delve into various strategies for generating passive income, including real estate investments, dividend stocks, peer-to-peer lending, online businesses, and more. By understanding the principles of passive income and implementing strategic investment strategies, you can create multiple streams of passive income that provide financial security and freedom for years to come.

Understanding Passive Income

Passive income is income that is earned with minimal effort or active involvement on the part of the recipient. Unlike earned income, which requires ongoing work or effort to generate, passive income streams continue to generate income even when you're not actively working. Passive income can take many forms, including rental income from real estate properties, dividends from stocks and investments, royalties from intellectual property, interest from savings accounts or bonds, and income from online businesses or affiliate marketing.

Benefits of Passive Income

Financial Freedom: Passive income provides financial freedom by enabling you to generate income without being tied to a specific job or location. This flexibility allows you to pursue other interests, spend time with family, or travel while still earning income passively.

Diversification: Creating multiple streams of passive income diversifies your income sources, reducing dependence on any single source of income. This diversification helps mitigate risk and provides stability during economic downturns or market fluctuations.

Scalability: Many passive income streams have the potential for scalability, meaning that you can increase your income exponentially over time with relatively little additional effort or investment. This scalability allows you to grow your passive income portfolio and achieve greater financial success.

Wealth Building: Passive income streams have the potential to generate significant wealth over time through compounding returns and appreciation. By reinvesting passive income into additional income-generating assets, you can accelerate wealth accumulation and achieve financial goals more quickly.

Strategies for Generating Passive Income

Real Estate Investing: Real estate investing is a popular strategy for generating passive income through rental properties, vacation rentals, or real estate crowdfunding platforms. Rental income from properties can provide a steady stream of passive income, while property appreciation can increase overall wealth over time.

Dividend Investing: Dividend investing involves purchasing stocks or funds that pay regular dividends to shareholders. Dividend income can provide a reliable source of passive income, with the potential for growth through dividend reinvestment and capital appreciation.

Peer-to-Peer Lending: Peer-to-peer lending platforms allow individuals to lend money to others in exchange for interest payments. By investing in peer-to-peer loans, you can earn passive income through interest payments without the need for active management.

Online Businesses: Online businesses such as e-commerce stores, affiliate marketing, and digital products can generate passive income through automated sales and recurring revenue streams. With the right systems and marketing strategies in place, online businesses can generate income 24/7 with minimal ongoing effort.

Royalties and Licensing: Royalties from intellectual property such as books, music, patents, or trademarks can provide passive income for creators and inventors. Licensing agreements allow individuals to earn passive income by allowing others to use their intellectual property in exchange for royalties or licensing fees.

Building a Passive Income Portfolio

Building a passive income portfolio involves diversifying your income streams and investing in a mix of assets that generate passive income. Start by assessing your financial goals, risk tolerance, and investment preferences to determine which passive income strategies are best suited to your needs. Consider consulting with a financial advisor or investment professional to develop a personalized investment plan tailored to your goals and circumstances.

Challenges and Considerations

While passive income offers many benefits, it's essential to recognize that building passive income streams requires time, effort, and careful planning. Some passive income strategies may involve upfront costs or risks, and not all passive income opportunities are created equal. It's crucial to conduct thorough research, due diligence, and risk assessment before investing in any passive income opportunity. Additionally, passive income is not entirely "set it and forget it," and some level of monitoring and management may be required to ensure the success of your passive income streams.

Conclusion

In conclusion, creating financial freedom through passive income is a achievable goal for those willing to invest time, effort, and resources into building multiple streams of passive income. By understanding the principles of passive income and implementing strategic investment strategies, you can generate reliable income streams that provide financial security and freedom for years to come. Whether through real estate investing, dividend stocks, peer-to-peer lending, online businesses, or other passive income opportunities, building a passive income portfolio can help you achieve your financial goals and live life on your own terms. Through careful planning, diversification, and ongoing management, you can create a path to financial freedom and build wealth for the future.

Chapter 13: Philanthropy and Giving Back: The True Essence of Wealth

Philanthropy and giving back are fundamental aspects of wealth that extend beyond financial success. In this chapter, we explore the transformative power of philanthropy in shaping communities, fostering social change, and enriching the lives of both givers and recipients. We delve into the various forms of philanthropy, from charitable donations and volunteer work to social entrepreneurship and impact investing. By understanding the true essence of wealth as the ability to make a positive impact on the world, we can harness the power of philanthropy to create meaningful change and leave a lasting legacy.

The Meaning of Philanthropy

Philanthropy is the act of promoting the welfare of others through charitable giving, volunteerism, or advocacy. At its core, philanthropy is about using one's resources, whether financial or otherwise, to make a positive impact on the lives of others and address pressing social issues. Philanthropy encompasses a wide range of activities, including donating money to charitable organizations, volunteering time and expertise to community projects, advocating for social justice and equity, and supporting causes that align with one's values and priorities.

The Impact of Philanthropy

Philanthropy has the power to create profound and lasting change in communities around the world. By addressing root causes of social issues such as poverty, inequality, education, and healthcare, philanthropy can help break the cycle of poverty, empower marginalized communities, and promote social justice and equity. Philanthropic efforts also support the arts, culture, and education, enriching the lives of individuals and fostering creativity, innovation, and lifelong learning. Moreover, philanthropy can inspire others to give back, creating a ripple effect of generosity and compassion that extends far beyond individual acts of kindness.

Forms of Philanthropy

Philanthropy takes many forms, each with its own unique impact and benefits:

Charitable Giving: Donating money to charitable organizations is one of the most common forms of philanthropy. Charitable donations support a wide range of causes, including education, healthcare, environmental conservation, and social services.

Volunteerism: Volunteering time and expertise to community organizations and projects is another important form of philanthropy. By donating their time and skills, volunteers can make a tangible difference in their communities and forge meaningful connections with others.

Social Entrepreneurship: Social entrepreneurship involves using business principles and strategies to address social or environmental challenges. Social entrepreneurs create innovative solutions to pressing issues while generating sustainable revenue to support their work.

Impact Investing: Impact investing involves making investments that generate both financial returns and positive social or environmental impact. Impact investors seek to align their investment portfolios with their values and priorities, supporting businesses and organizations that create positive change.

Advocacy and Activism: Advocacy and activism involve raising awareness about social issues, advocating for policy changes, and mobilizing others to take action. Advocates and activists play a critical role in driving social change and addressing systemic injustices.

The Benefits of Philanthropy

Philanthropy offers numerous benefits for both givers and recipients:

Personal Fulfillment: Giving back can bring a sense of purpose, meaning, and fulfillment to your life. Knowing that you are making a positive difference in the lives of others can enhance your overall well-being and sense of happiness.

Connection and Community: Philanthropy fosters connections with others who share your values and commitment to making a difference. By joining forces with like-minded individuals and organizations, you can amplify your impact and create meaningful change together.

Legacy and Impact: Philanthropy allows you to leave a lasting legacy that extends far beyond your lifetime. By supporting causes that are meaningful to you, you can make a positive impact on future generations and create a better world for years to come.

Social Responsibility: Philanthropy reflects a sense of social responsibility and stewardship towards others and the planet. By giving back to those in need and supporting efforts to address social and environmental challenges, you contribute to the greater good and help create a more just and sustainable world.

Cultivating a Culture of Philanthropy

Cultivating a culture of philanthropy involves fostering a spirit of generosity, compassion, and social responsibility within individuals, families, organizations, and communities. Here are some ways to cultivate a culture of philanthropy:

Lead by Example: Lead by example and demonstrate your commitment to giving back through your actions and words. Share your philanthropic experiences and encourage others to get involved.

Educate and Inspire: Educate others about the importance of philanthropy and the impact it can have on individuals and communities. Share stories of philanthropic success and inspire others to take action.

Foster Collaboration: Foster collaboration and partnerships among individuals, organizations, and sectors to maximize impact and address complex social challenges collectively.

Celebrate Generosity: Celebrate generosity and recognize the contributions of individuals and organizations who give back to their communities. Express gratitude for the support of donors, volunteers, and advocates.

Empower Future Generations: Empower future generations to become philanthropic leaders by instilling values of generosity, empathy, and social responsibility from a young age. Encourage young people to get involved in philanthropy and support causes that are meaningful to them.

Conclusion

In conclusion, philanthropy and giving back are essential components of wealth that extend beyond financial success. By harnessing the power of philanthropy, individuals, families, organizations, and communities can make a positive impact on the world and leave a lasting legacy of compassion, generosity, and social responsibility. Whether through charitable giving, volunteerism, social entrepreneurship, impact investing, or advocacy, everyone has the power to make a difference and create positive change in the world. Through collective action and a shared commitment to the greater good, we can build a more equitable, just, and sustainable future for all.

Chapter 14: Mastering Money Management Skills

Mastering money management skills is essential for achieving financial stability, security, and success. In this chapter, we explore the key principles and strategies for effective money management, including budgeting, saving, investing, debt management, and financial planning. By developing strong money management skills and habits, you can take control of your finances, achieve your financial goals, and build a solid foundation for long-term wealth and prosperity.

Understanding Money Management

Money management is the process of effectively managing your finances to achieve financial goals and priorities. It involves making informed decisions about earning, spending, saving, investing, and budgeting to optimize your financial resources and maximize financial well-being. Effective money management requires discipline, planning, and a clear understanding of your financial situation, goals, and priorities.

Setting Financial Goals

The first step in effective money management is setting clear, achievable financial goals. Financial goals provide a roadmap for your financial journey and help guide your decisions and priorities. Whether your goals include saving for retirement, buying a home, paying off debt, or starting a business, having specific, measurable goals gives you direction and motivation to take action and make progress towards your objectives.

Creating a Budget

A budget is a foundational tool for effective money management, helping you track income, expenses, and savings to ensure that you're living within your means and making progress towards your financial goals. To create a budget:

Identify Income: Determine your total monthly income from all sources, including salary, wages, freelance income, investment income, and other sources.

Track Expenses: Track your expenses over a set period (e.g., one month) to identify where your money is going. Categorize expenses into fixed (e.g., rent, utilities) and variable (e.g., groceries, entertainment) expenses.

Set Spending Priorities: Allocate your income towards essential expenses, savings, debt repayment, and discretionary spending based on your financial goals and priorities. Monitor and Adjust: Regularly review your budget to track your progress, identify areas for improvement, and make adjustments as needed to stay on track.

Saving and Emergency Fund

Saving is a fundamental aspect of money management, providing a financial cushion for unexpected expenses, achieving financial goals, and building long-term wealth. Establishing an emergency fund is a critical component of saving, providing a financial safety net to cover unexpected expenses such as medical bills, car repairs, or job loss. Aim to save three to six months' worth of living expenses in an easily accessible savings account to provide financial security and peace of mind.

Managing Debt

Debt management is another key aspect of effective money management, as excessive debt can hinder your financial progress and limit your options. To manage debt effectively:

Prioritize High-Interest Debt: Focus on paying off high-interest debt first, such as credit card debt or payday loans, to minimize interest charges and accelerate debt repayment.

Consolidate Debt: Consider consolidating multiple debts into a single loan with a lower interest rate to simplify repayment and reduce overall interest costs.

Develop a Repayment Plan: Create a debt repayment plan that outlines how much you'll pay towards each debt each month, prioritizing high-interest debt while maintaining minimum payments on other debts.

Avoid Accumulating New Debt: Take steps to avoid accumulating new debt by living within your means, budgeting wisely, and practicing responsible spending habits.

Investing for the Future

Investing is a powerful wealth-building tool that can help you achieve long-term financial goals such as retirement, education, or financial independence. To invest effectively:

Set Investment Goals: Define your investment goals, time horizon, and risk tolerance to determine the appropriate investment strategy for your needs.

Diversify Your Portfolio: Diversification is key to managing risk and maximizing returns. Spread your investments across different asset classes (e.g., stocks, bonds, real estate) and geographic regions to reduce exposure to any single investment.

Invest Regularly: Consistent, disciplined investing over time can help you take advantage of compounding returns and achieve your long-term financial goals.

Monitor and Rebalance: Regularly review your investment portfolio to ensure it remains aligned with your goals and risk tolerance. Rebalance your portfolio as needed to maintain diversification and manage risk.

Financial Planning and Retirement

Financial planning is the process of setting financial goals, creating a plan to achieve them, and regularly reviewing and adjusting your plan as needed. Retirement planning is a critical aspect of financial planning, ensuring that you have the resources and income needed to maintain your desired lifestyle in retirement. To plan for retirement effectively:

Determine Retirement Goals: Estimate your retirement expenses and income needs to determine how much you'll need to save for retirement.

Save Consistently: Start saving for retirement as early as possible and contribute regularly to retirement accounts such as 401(k)s, IRAs, or pension plans to take advantage of tax benefits and employer matches.

Consider Long-Term Care: Factor in potential long-term care needs when planning for retirement, including healthcare costs, insurance coverage, and estate planning.

Seek Professional Advice: Consider working with a financial advisor or retirement planner to develop a personalized retirement plan tailored to your goals, risk tolerance, and financial situation.

Conclusion

In conclusion, mastering money management skills is essential for achieving financial stability, security, and success. By setting clear financial goals, creating a budget, saving regularly, managing debt effectively, investing wisely, and planning for retirement, you can take control of your finances and build a solid foundation for long-term wealth and prosperity. Effective money management requires discipline, planning, and a commitment to making informed financial decisions that align with your goals and priorities. Through proactive financial management and ongoing education, you can achieve financial freedom and create the life you desire.

Chapter 15: The Power of Visualization and Manifestation in Wealth Creation

Visualization and manifestation are powerful tools that can help individuals achieve their financial goals and create abundance in their lives. In this chapter, we explore the principles of visualization and manifestation and how they can be applied to wealth creation. We delve into techniques for harnessing the power of the mind to attract prosperity, abundance, and financial success. By understanding the principles of visualization and manifestation and incorporating them into your daily life, you can unlock your full potential and create the wealth and abundance you desire.

Understanding Visualization and Manifestation

Visualization is the practice of creating mental images or scenes of desired outcomes or goals. By vividly imagining yourself achieving your goals and experiencing the emotions associated with success, you can activate the subconscious mind and align your thoughts, beliefs, and actions with your desired outcomes. Manifestation is the process of bringing your desires and intentions into reality through focused attention, belief, and action. By harnessing the power of intention and belief, you can manifest your desires and create the life you envision.

The Law of Attraction

Central to the principles of visualization and manifestation is the Law of Attraction, which states that like attracts like. According to the Law of Attraction, your thoughts, beliefs, and emotions create energetic vibrations that attract similar vibrations into your life. By focusing on positive thoughts, beliefs, and emotions, you can attract positive experiences, opportunities, and abundance into your life. Conversely, focusing on negative thoughts and beliefs can attract negative experiences and limitations.

Techniques for Visualization and Manifestation

Create a Vision Board: A vision board is a visual representation of your goals, dreams, and desires. Create a collage of images, words, and affirmations that represent your ideal life and the goals you want to manifest. Place your vision board in a prominent location where you can see it daily and visualize yourself living your desired reality.

Practice Creative Visualization: Set aside time each day to practice creative visualization. Close your eyes and imagine yourself achieving your goals in vivid detail, using all of your senses to make the experience as real as possible. Visualize yourself experiencing the emotions of success and abundance, and hold onto those feelings as you go about your day.

Use Affirmations: Affirmations are positive statements that reinforce your beliefs and intentions. Create affirmations that affirm your wealth, abundance, and success, and repeat them regularly throughout the day. Affirmations can help reprogram your subconscious mind and align your thoughts and beliefs with your desired outcomes.

Practice Gratitude: Cultivate an attitude of gratitude for the abundance and blessings in your life. Take time each day to express gratitude for the wealth and abundance you already have, as well as the wealth and abundance that is on its way to you. Gratitude raises your vibration and opens you up to receiving more blessings and abundance.

Take Inspired Action: While visualization and manifestation are powerful tools, they must be accompanied by inspired action to bring your desires into reality. Take consistent, focused action towards your goals, and remain open to opportunities and synchronicities that come your way. Trust that the universe is conspiring in your favor and that everything you need to achieve your goals will be provided to you.

Overcoming Limiting Beliefs

One of the biggest obstacles to visualization and manifestation is limiting beliefs, which are negative thoughts or beliefs that undermine your confidence and self-esteem. Common limiting beliefs related to wealth and abundance include beliefs about money being scarce, beliefs about not deserving wealth, and beliefs about not being capable of achieving financial success. To overcome limiting beliefs:

Identify Limiting Beliefs: Take time to identify any limiting beliefs you may have about wealth and abundance. Pay attention to negative thoughts and self-talk related to money, success, and abundance.

Challenge Your Beliefs: Challenge your limiting beliefs by questioning their validity and considering alternative perspectives. Ask yourself if your beliefs are based on facts or assumptions, and consider how they may be holding you back from achieving your goals. Replace Limiting Beliefs with Empowering Beliefs: Replace limiting beliefs with empowering beliefs that support your goals and aspirations. Affirmations and positive self-talk can help reprogram your subconscious mind and instill new, empowering beliefs about wealth and abundance.

Visualize Success: Use visualization techniques to visualize yourself overcoming obstacles, achieving your goals, and experiencing abundance in your life. Focus on the feelings of confidence, empowerment, and success that accompany your visualizations, and hold onto those feelings as you take inspired action towards your goals.

The Power of Persistence and Patience

Visualization and manifestation require patience, persistence, and trust in the process. Rome wasn't built in a day, and neither are your dreams and goals. Be patient with yourself and the universe, and trust that everything is unfolding in divine timing. Stay committed to your vision, take consistent action towards your goals, and remain open to receiving abundance in all its forms. Remember that the universe is infinitely abundant, and there is more than enough wealth and abundance for everyone.

Conclusion

In conclusion, visualization and manifestation are powerful tools for creating wealth, abundance, and success in your life. By harnessing the power of your mind and aligning your thoughts, beliefs, and actions with your desired outcomes, you can attract prosperity, abundance, and financial success into your life. Practice creative visualization, use affirmations, cultivate gratitude, and take inspired action towards your goals. Overcome limiting beliefs, be patient and persistent, and trust in the process. Remember that you have the power to create the life of your dreams, and that abundance is your birthright. Through the practice of visualization and manifestation, you can unlock your full potential and create the wealth and abundance you desire.

Chapter 16: Thriving in Economic Turbulence: Strategies for Financial Resilience

In times of economic turbulence and uncertainty, building financial resilience is essential for navigating challenges, weathering storms, and thriving despite adversity. In this chapter, we explore strategies for building financial resilience, including emergency preparedness, diversification, debt management, budgeting, and ongoing education. By implementing these strategies and cultivating a resilient mindset, you can strengthen your financial foundation, mitigate risks, and thrive in the face of economic uncertainty.

Understanding Financial Resilience

Financial resilience is the ability to withstand and recover from financial setbacks, disruptions, and crises. It involves building a strong financial foundation, developing effective money management skills, and adopting a mindset of adaptability and resourcefulness. Financially resilient individuals are better equipped to navigate economic turbulence, overcome challenges, and bounce back from setbacks stronger than before.

Emergency Preparedness

One of the cornerstones of financial resilience is emergency preparedness. Building an emergency fund is essential for providing a financial safety net to cover unexpected expenses, such as medical bills, car repairs, or job loss. Aim to save three to six months' worth of living expenses in an easily accessible savings account to provide peace of mind and financial security during times of crisis.

Diversification

Diversification is another key component of financial resilience, as it helps spread risk and minimize exposure to any single asset or investment. Diversify your investment portfolio across different asset classes, industries, and geographic regions to reduce the impact of market fluctuations and economic downturns. Consider investing in a mix of stocks, bonds, real estate, and alternative investments to create a well-balanced and resilient portfolio.

Debt Management

Effective debt management is crucial for building financial resilience and avoiding excessive financial strain. Prioritize paying off high-interest debt first, such as credit card debt or payday loans, to minimize interest charges and accelerate debt repayment. Consider consolidating multiple debts into a single loan with a lower interest rate to simplify repayment and reduce overall interest costs. Develop a repayment plan and budget to ensure that you're making consistent progress towards debt elimination while maintaining your other financial goals and priorities.

Budgeting

Budgeting is a fundamental money management skill that is essential for building financial resilience. Create a budget that outlines your income, expenses, savings, and financial goals to ensure that you're living within your means and making progress towards your objectives. Track your spending, identify areas for improvement, and make adjustments as needed to stay on track with your financial plan. Budgeting helps you prioritize your spending, build savings, and prepare for unexpected expenses, thereby enhancing your overall financial resilience.

Ongoing Education

Continuous learning and education are essential for building financial resilience and adapting to changing economic conditions. Stay informed about economic trends, financial markets, and personal finance topics by reading books, attending seminars, and following reputable financial news sources. Take advantage of educational resources and tools available online to enhance your financial literacy and empower yourself to make informed financial decisions. By staying informed and proactive, you can better navigate economic turbulence and position yourself for long-term financial success.

Cultivating a Resilient Mindset

In addition to practical strategies, cultivating a resilient mindset is essential for building financial resilience. Cultivate qualities such as adaptability, flexibility, and resourcefulness to navigate challenges and setbacks with confidence and determination. Embrace change as an opportunity for growth and learning, and maintain a positive outlook even in the face of adversity. By cultivating a resilient mindset, you can overcome obstacles, persevere through difficult times, and emerge stronger and more resilient than before.

Conclusion

In conclusion, thriving in economic turbulence requires building financial resilience through strategic planning, prudent decision-making, and a resilient mindset. By implementing strategies such as emergency preparedness, diversification, debt management, budgeting, and ongoing education, you can strengthen your financial foundation, mitigate risks, and thrive in the face of uncertainty. Cultivate qualities such as adaptability, flexibility, and resourcefulness to navigate challenges with confidence and determination. Remember that building financial resilience is a journey, not a destination, and that continuous learning, adaptation, and growth are essential for long-term success. Through proactive planning, prudent decision-making, and a resilient mindset, you can build a brighter financial future and thrive in any economic environment.

Chapter 17: Answering Your Top 30 Money Questions

Money can be a complex and challenging topic, with many questions and concerns that arise as individuals strive to manage their finances effectively. In this chapter, we address some of the most common and pressing money questions that people often have. From budgeting and saving to investing and retirement planning, we provide clear, informative answers to help you make informed decisions and achieve financial success.

1. How do I create a budget that works for me?

Creating a budget starts with understanding your income, expenses, and financial goals. Begin by tracking your spending and categorizing your expenses. Then, allocate your income towards essential expenses, savings, debt repayment, and discretionary spending based on your priorities. Regularly review and adjust your budget as needed to ensure that it aligns with your financial goals and lifestyle.

2. What are some effective strategies for saving money?

Effective strategies for saving money include automating your savings, setting specific savings goals, reducing discretionary spending, and prioritizing your financial goals. Consider implementing the 50/30/20 budgeting rule, which allocates 50% of your income to needs, 30% to wants, and 20% to savings and debt repayment.

3. How can I get out of debt and start building wealth?

To get out of debt and start building wealth, focus on paying off high-interest debt first, such as credit card debt or payday loans. Develop a debt repayment plan that outlines how much you'll pay towards each debt each month, prioritizing high-interest debt while maintaining minimum payments on other debts. Once you're debt-free, focus on building an emergency fund, investing for the future, and increasing your income to accelerate wealth-building.

4. What are some common investing mistakes to avoid?

Common investing mistakes to avoid include investing based on emotions, neglecting to diversify your portfolio, trying to time the market, and chasing hot investment trends. Instead, focus on long-term investing strategies, diversify your investments across different asset classes, and stick to your investment plan regardless of short-term market fluctuations.

5. How much should I save for retirement?

The amount you should save for retirement depends on factors such as your age, income, lifestyle, and retirement goals. A general rule of thumb is to aim to replace 70-90% of your pre-retirement income in retirement. Calculate your retirement savings goal based on your expected expenses in retirement and your desired retirement age, and work towards saving that amount over time.

6. What are the different types of retirement accounts available?

There are several types of retirement accounts available, including employer-sponsored plans such as 401(k)s and 403(b)s, individual retirement accounts (IRAs), Roth IRAs, and self-employed retirement plans such as SEP IRAs and Solo 401(k)s. Each type of retirement account has its own contribution limits, tax advantages, and eligibility requirements, so it's essential to understand your options and choose the best retirement accounts for your needs.

7. How can I protect my finances in case of unexpected emergencies?

To protect your finances in case of unexpected emergencies, establish an emergency fund with three to six months' worth of living expenses in a liquid savings account. Review your insurance coverage, including health insurance, disability insurance, life insurance, and property insurance, to ensure that you're adequately protected against unexpected events. Additionally, consider establishing a power of attorney and healthcare directive to designate someone to make financial and medical decisions on your behalf if you become incapacitated.

8. What are some smart strategies for negotiating a salary or raise?

Smart strategies for negotiating a salary or raise include researching salary benchmarks for your industry and location, quantifying your achievements and contributions to the organization, practicing effective communication and negotiation skills, and being prepared to advocate for yourself confidently. Consider negotiating other benefits such as flexible work arrangements, additional vacation time, or professional development opportunities if a higher salary isn't feasible.

9. How can I improve my credit score?

Improving your credit score involves managing your credit responsibly and taking steps to demonstrate creditworthiness to lenders. Pay your bills on time, keep your credit card balances low, avoid opening new credit accounts unnecessarily, and monitor your credit report regularly for errors or inaccuracies. Over time, responsible credit management can help improve your credit score and qualify you for better interest rates and loan terms.

10. What are some effective ways to teach children about money?

Effective ways to teach children about money include leading by example, involving children in financial discussions and decision-making, setting up a savings account for them to manage, and providing age-appropriate lessons about budgeting, saving, spending, and giving. Use real-life experiences such as grocery shopping or saving for a goal to teach children practical money skills and instill good financial habits from a young age.

11. How can I maximize my tax deductions and credits?

To maximize your tax deductions and credits, take advantage of available tax breaks such as retirement account contributions, mortgage interest deductions, charitable donations, and education-related expenses. Consider consulting with a tax professional or using tax preparation software to ensure that you're taking advantage of all available deductions and credits and minimizing your tax liability.

12. What are some effective strategies for managing investment risk?

Effective strategies for managing investment risk include diversifying your investment portfolio, investing for the long term, periodically rebalancing your portfolio to maintain your desired asset allocation, and staying informed about economic trends and market conditions. Consider your risk tolerance, investment goals, and time horizon when designing your investment strategy, and be prepared to adjust your portfolio as needed to manage risk effectively.

13. How can I start investing with a small amount of money?

You can start investing with a small amount of money by opening a brokerage account with a low minimum investment requirement, investing in low-cost index funds or exchange-traded funds (ETFs), and taking advantage of commission-free trading platforms. Consider investing regularly through dollar-cost averaging, which involves investing a fixed amount of money at regular intervals regardless of market fluctuations, to build wealth over time.

14. What are some smart strategies for paying for college?

Smart strategies for paying for college include saving early and often in a tax-advantaged college savings account such as a 529 plan, exploring scholarship and grant opportunities, maximizing federal student aid by completing the Free Application for Federal Student Aid (FAFSA), considering community college or in-state public universities to reduce costs, and encouraging students to work part-time or pursue paid internships to offset expenses.

15. How can I protect my investments from inflation?

To protect your investments from inflation, consider investing in assets that have historically provided a hedge against inflation, such as stocks, real estate, and commodities. Maintain a diversified investment portfolio with exposure to different asset classes and geographic regions to spread risk and mitigate the impact of inflation on your overall investment portfolio. Additionally, consider investing in Treasury Inflation-Protected Securities (TIPS), which are designed to protect against inflation by adjusting their principal value based on changes in the Consumer Price Index (CPI).

16. What are some effective strategies for negotiating lower interest rates on loans or credit cards?

Effective strategies for negotiating lower interest rates on loans or credit cards include researching current interest rates, comparing offers from different lenders, improving your credit score, demonstrating a history of responsible credit management, and negotiating with your current lender based on your creditworthiness and relationship with the institution. Consider refinancing high-interest loans or transferring credit card balances to a lower-interest card to reduce interest costs and save money over time.

17. How can I start a successful side hustle or freelance business?

To start a successful side hustle or freelance business, identify your skills, interests, and passions, and explore potential business ideas that align with your strengths and expertise. Develop a business plan that outlines your target market, products or services, pricing strategy, marketing plan, and financial projections. Leverage online platforms and social media to promote your business and attract clients or customers, and be prepared to invest time and effort into building and growing your venture.

18. What are some effective strategies for negotiating lower prices on purchases?

Effective strategies for negotiating lower prices on purchases include doing your research and comparing prices from multiple retailers, leveraging price-matching policies and coupons, negotiating bulk discounts or package deals, being polite and respectful during negotiations, and being prepared to walk away if you're unable to reach a mutually beneficial agreement. Consider purchasing items during sales or promotional periods to take advantage of discounts and savings opportunities.

19. How can I start planning for retirement if I'm self-employed?

If you're self-employed, you can start planning for retirement by setting up a tax-advantaged retirement account such as a SEP IRA, Solo 401(k), or SIMPLE IRA. These retirement accounts offer tax benefits and flexibility for self-employed individuals to save for retirement and reduce their taxable income. Consider working with a financial advisor or retirement planner to determine the best retirement savings strategy for your unique needs and circumstances.

20. What are some effective strategies for negotiating a lease or rental agreement?

Effective strategies for negotiating a lease or rental agreement include researching rental rates and market trends in your area, identifying any issues or concerns with the property that could be used as leverage during negotiations, being prepared to negotiate terms such as rent price, lease duration, and pet policies, and documenting any agreements or concessions in writing. Consider working with a real estate agent or attorney to help negotiate favorable terms and protect your interests.

21. How can I protect my assets and estate for future generations?

To protect your assets and estate for future generations, consider establishing a comprehensive estate plan that includes a will, trust, power of attorney, and healthcare directive. Review your beneficiary designations regularly and update them as needed to ensure that your assets are distributed according to your wishes. Consider working with an estate planning attorney or financial advisor to develop a personalized estate plan that addresses your unique goals and circumstances.

22. What are some effective strategies for negotiating a job offer or promotion?

Effective strategies for negotiating a job offer or promotion include researching salary benchmarks and industry standards for your position, quantifying your achievements and contributions to the organization, practicing effective negotiation and communication skills, and being prepared to walk away if the offer doesn't meet your expectations. Consider negotiating other benefits such as flexible work arrangements, additional vacation time, or professional development opportunities if a higher salary isn't feasible.

23. How can I protect myself from identity theft and fraud?

To protect yourself from identity theft and fraud, safeguard your personal information and financial accounts by using strong, unique passwords, monitoring your credit report regularly for suspicious activity, being cautious about sharing personal information online or over the phone, and shredding sensitive documents before discarding them. Consider enrolling in identity theft protection services or credit monitoring services for added security and peace of mind.

24. What are some effective strategies for negotiating medical bills or healthcare expenses?

Effective strategies for negotiating medical bills or healthcare expenses include reviewing your medical bills carefully for errors or discrepancies, asking for an itemized bill to understand charges, negotiating discounts or payment plans with healthcare providers, and seeking financial assistance or charity care programs if you're unable to afford your medical bills. Consider hiring a medical billing advocate or negotiating with your insurance company to reduce out-of-pocket expenses and save money on healthcare costs.

25. How can I build credit history and establish a good credit score?

To build credit history and establish a good credit score, start by applying for a secured credit card or becoming an authorized user on someone else's credit card account. Use credit responsibly by making timely payments, keeping your credit card balances low, and avoiding opening new credit accounts unnecessarily. Monitor your credit report regularly for errors or inaccuracies, and take steps to correct any issues that could negatively impact your credit score.

26. What are some effective strategies for negotiating lower insurance premiums?

Effective strategies for negotiating lower insurance premiums include shopping around and comparing quotes from multiple insurance providers, bundling multiple insurance policies with the same provider for discounts, raising your deductibles or coverage limits to lower your premiums, and asking about available discounts for factors such as good driving habits, home security features, or membership in professional organizations. Consider working with an independent insurance agent or broker to help you find the best coverage at the lowest price.

27. How can I protect my investments from market volatility and economic downturns?

To protect your investments from market volatility and economic downturns, maintain a diversified investment portfolio with exposure to different asset classes, industries, and geographic regions. Consider allocating a portion of your portfolio to defensive investments such as bonds, cash equivalents, or defensive stocks that are less sensitive to market fluctuations. Avoid making impulsive investment decisions based on short-term market movements, and focus on your long-term investment goals and objectives.

28. What are some effective strategies for negotiating lower interest rates on mortgages or refinancing?

Effective strategies for negotiating lower interest rates on mortgages or refinancing include improving your credit score, shopping around and comparing offers from multiple lenders, considering different loan terms and repayment options, and being prepared to negotiate based on your creditworthiness and financial situation. Consider paying discount points upfront to lower your interest rate, and be sure to factor in all associated closing costs and fees when evaluating loan offers.

29. How can I start a successful investment portfolio with limited funds?

You can start a successful investment portfolio with limited funds by focusing on low-cost, diversified investments such as index funds or ETFs that offer exposure to a broad range of assets. Consider investing regularly through automatic investment plans or fractional investing platforms that allow you to purchase fractional shares of stocks or ETFs with small amounts of money. Over time, continue to contribute to your investment portfolio and reinvest dividends to grow your wealth gradually.

30. What are some effective strategies for negotiating lower fees or expenses with financial institutions?

Effective strategies for negotiating lower fees or expenses with financial institutions include researching fee schedules and expense ratios for comparable products or services, leveraging competitive offers from other institutions as leverage during negotiations, demonstrating a history of loyalty and positive account activity, and being prepared to switch to a different provider if your current institution isn't willing to accommodate your requests. Consider negotiating package deals or bundling multiple services together for discounts, and don't be afraid to ask for fee waivers or reductions based on your relationship with the institution.

Conclusion

In conclusion, addressing your top 30 money questions requires a combination of financial knowledge, practical skills, and effective communication. By understanding key concepts such as budgeting, saving, investing, and retirement planning, and implementing smart strategies for managing your finances, you can make informed decisions and achieve your financial goals. Remember to stay informed, be proactive, and seek professional advice when needed to navigate complex financial situations and make the most of your money. With dedication, perseverance, and a commitment to lifelong learning, you can build a solid financial foundation and create the life you desire.

Chapter 18: Embracing a Wealthy Mindset: Cultivating Abundance in Every Area of Your Life

Embracing a wealthy mindset goes beyond mere financial success; it encompasses a holistic approach to abundance in every aspect of life. In this chapter, we delve into the principles of a wealthy mindset and explore strategies for cultivating abundance in areas such as relationships, health, personal growth, and contribution to society. By adopting a wealthy mindset, you can unlock your full potential, attract prosperity, and create a life of fulfillment and abundance.

Understanding a Wealthy Mindset

A wealthy mindset is a mindset of abundance, prosperity, and gratitude. It involves shifting your perspective from scarcity and limitation to abundance and possibility. Instead of focusing on what you lack or what's missing, a wealthy mindset focuses on what you have and what's possible. It involves believing in your own worthiness and deservingness of abundance in all areas of life and being open to receiving the blessings and opportunities that come your way.

Cultivating Gratitude

Gratitude is a cornerstone of a wealthy mindset. By cultivating an attitude of gratitude, you can shift your focus from what you lack to what you have, thereby attracting more blessings and abundance into your life. Practice gratitude daily by keeping a gratitude journal, expressing appreciation for the people and things in your life, and focusing on the positive aspects of every situation. Gratitude opens your heart and mind to the abundance that surrounds you and aligns you with the flow of blessings and opportunities.

Aligning with Your Values

Living a wealthy life means living in alignment with your values and priorities. Take time to identify your core values and what matters most to you in life. Then, align your thoughts, beliefs, and actions with your values and make decisions that are in line with your priorities. When you live authentically and in alignment with your values, you create a sense of fulfillment and abundance that transcends material wealth.

Investing in Relationships

Relationships are a vital component of a wealthy life. Cultivate meaningful connections with family, friends, and loved ones, and invest time and energy into nurturing those relationships. Practice active listening, empathy, and compassion, and prioritize quality time spent together. Surround yourself with people who uplift and support you on your journey, and be a source of encouragement and inspiration for others. Building strong relationships enriches your life and adds depth and meaning to your experiences.

Prioritizing Health and Well-being

True wealth encompasses health and well-being in addition to material prosperity. Prioritize your physical, mental, and emotional health by adopting healthy lifestyle habits such as regular exercise, nutritious eating, adequate sleep, and stress management techniques. Make self-care a priority and listen to your body's signals and needs. Invest in activities and practices that nourish your soul and bring you joy, whether it's spending time in nature, practicing mindfulness, or pursuing creative hobbies.

Committing to Personal Growth

Personal growth is essential for living a wealthy life. Commit to lifelong learning and self-improvement by seeking out opportunities for growth and development. Set goals that stretch and challenge you, and be willing to step outside of your comfort zone in pursuit of your dreams. Embrace failure as a learning opportunity and use setbacks as stepping stones to success. Cultivate a growth mindset that sees obstacles as temporary setbacks and believes in your ability to overcome challenges and achieve your goals.

Contributing to Society

A wealthy life isn't just about accumulating wealth for yourself; it's also about making a positive impact on the world around you. Find ways to contribute to society and give back to others, whether through volunteering, philanthropy, or acts of kindness. Use your time, talents, and resources to make a difference in the lives of others and create positive change in your community and beyond. By contributing to the greater good, you not only enrich the lives of others but also experience a sense of fulfillment and purpose that money alone cannot provide.

Practicing Abundance Consciousness

Abundance consciousness is the belief that the universe is infinitely abundant and that there is more than enough wealth, resources, and opportunities for everyone. By practicing abundance consciousness, you shift your focus from scarcity and lack to abundance and possibility. Cultivate an abundance mindset by affirming your worthiness and deservingness of abundance, visualizing your goals and desires as already manifested, and trusting in the divine flow of abundance in your life. When you align your thoughts, beliefs, and actions with abundance consciousness, you open yourself up to the unlimited possibilities and opportunities that surround you.

Conclusion

In conclusion, embracing a wealthy mindset is about more than just accumulating material wealth; it's about cultivating abundance in every area of your life. By adopting a mindset of gratitude, aligning with your values, investing in relationships, prioritizing health and well-being, committing to personal growth, contributing to society, and practicing abundance consciousness, you can create a life of fulfillment, joy, and abundance. Remember that true wealth lies not in what you have but in who you are and how you choose to live your life. By embracing a wealthy mindset, you can unlock your full potential and create a life of abundance, prosperity, and purpose.

KEEP LEARNING, KEEP GROWING

THANK YOU

www.ingramcontent.com/pod-product-compliance
Lightning Source LLC
Chambersburg PA
CBHW082344270726
48658CB00017B/3113